What's the worst that could happen?

A Play

Based on the Daniel Spargo-Mabbs' Story

by

Mark Harrington

Copyright

2

For Jack

The brave friend who taught me all about
Daniel and trusted me with their friendship.

Contents

The Daniel Spargo-Mabbs Foundation (DSMF)

The Daniel Spargo-Mabbs Foundation (DSMF)

The DSM Foundation is a drug and alcohol education charity set up by Dan's parents Tim and Fiona. It aims to support young people to make safer choices and reduce harm through increasing their understanding of the effects and risks of drugs and alcohol by providing:

- evidence-based workshops and presentations to young people (11-18);
- Youth Ambassadors programme
- workshops for parents and carers;
- CPD training to teachers and professionals.

The workshops and presentations are supported by a comprehensive, on-line PHSRE programme available from www.dsmfoundation.org.uk.

The Foundation also commissioned a powerful verbatim play telling Dan's story from award-winning playwright Mark Wheeler: *'I Love You Mum – I Promise I Won't Die.'* (Bloomsbury, 2017). This play has been studied and performed around the world and has been touring schools since 2017 as a professional Theatre in Education production, with performances followed by interactive workshops. Since September 2022 it has been a GCSE Drama set text on the Eduqas syllabus.

The organisation is committed to diversity and differentiating its resources to provide access to people of all abilities. Therefore, it commissioned Mark Harrington to write this adapted play and a picture book which is supported by a drug education PHSRE programme for SEND students also available from the DSMF website.

DSMF works both in the UK and overseas and in addition to its drug education programme provides policy support and advice to external agencies. The Foundation is committed to further developing its resources and providing guidance and support. Therefore, it welcomes the opportunity to work with a range of individuals, schools, and organisation. For more information on the Foundation's work or to donate please visit: www.dsmfoundation.org.uk.

What's the worst that could happen?

Cast List

Jack (narrator) - Ben's friend 17 year-old

Ben - 17-year-old

Mia - 17-year-old

Jordon - Male/Female 17 year-old

Taylor - Male/Female 17 year-old

Charlie - Male/Female 17 year-old

Ali - Male/Female 17 year-old

Mum

Dad - Non-speaking

Brother - Non-speaking

Teacher - Male/Female

Bouncer

First Aider

Doctor - Non-speaking

10 ravers

The teenage and adult roles can be doubled up depending on the size of the group.

Scene 1: One moment can change everything.

Darkness. A slow heartbeat increases in speed over the scene. A train sound is heard getting closer and closer. As the lights come up, a circle of teenagers is on stage: Jordon, Taylor Charlie Ali, Jack and Ben.

Jordon: Guys, we're really doing this?

Ben: I'm not sure... I...

Taylor: Stop being such a baby!

Charlie: It's good stuff, I promise

Everyone except Ben is holding a 1.5 litre bottle of water in his or her hand. Ben has a 500 ml bottle.

Ali: We're all going to do it. Come on!

Ben: Okay! Okay!

The group cheers

Jack: Are you sure you want to do this?

Ben: Come on Jack. What's the worst that could happen?

The group all swig from their drinks, except for Jack who watches. As their bottles come away from their mouths, it goes dark and a

rewind/reverse sound is heard. This is
interrupted by a loud knocking.

Scene 2: Robin and his Batman

The stage right is laid out with a bed and a
nightstand lamp. On the nightstand is a mobile
phone; inside the drawer is a bottle of
aftershave. On the bed is a game controller.
This will show Ben's room. To stage left there is
a door. Jack is banging on the door. On the
other side Ben is getting ready to go out.

Jack: Ben, hurry up! I need a piss!

Ben: You can't rush a work of art!

Jack: Come on, you've been in there for hours!
Everyone will be wondering where we are.

Ben: I'll be two minutes.

Jack saunters over to Ben's bed and takes the
controller and begins playing. Muffled games
sounds are heard. Ben continues to prep
himself.

Jack: That guy in there is my best mate. The
myth, the legend that is Ben. Ben has been my
mate ever since we met in year ten. You know
what it's like, first day at a new school. Awkward.

But as soon as I met Ben he made me laugh and we've been mates ever since.

Jack looks at his phone

Jack: (*shouting towards Ben*) Ali's already at the station!

Ben: (*shouting back*) Hold on!

Ben begins to act out what Jack says to the following.

Jack: I always looked up to Ben. He was always so confident. Everybody liked him. When the big man upstairs was designing me, he must have been having an off day. You can literally play dot to dot with my face some days. Ben was like an action figure! Not a blemish, and all the girls fancied him.

Leaning into the audience whispering slightly.

He had a girlfriend and they snogged in the back row of the cinema.

Jack returns to normal voice.

Girls just seemed to run in the opposite direction when they saw me. Ben said his girlfriend had a mate who fancied me and next time they go out we can go on a double date. Best wing man right there! But this never happened. Anyway the girls at our school are just weird. Ergh, school! Don't get me started on school.

The bathroom now seems to change. Ben sits at a desk. A teacher enters.

For me school was always so hard - middle sets, extra work, tutors, resits.

Ben acts out doing tests and teacher marking.

But for Ben it was so easy...

Teacher: Well done Ben. That's an A star for English, A star for Maths, A star for History. Look they're all A star.

Jack: He was so popular that this happened...

Teacher takes an envelope out of his pocket. Sound effect drum roll.

Teacher: And now the moment we've been waiting for...This year's prom king is... Ben!

Teacher places a crown on his head. The teacher is in awe of touching Ben. Ben throws the crown down .

Jack: He was a master of selfies and his Facebook and Insta were filled with the most random places and people he had met.

Seriously, Ben was the nicest guy in the world, he helped in the community, and with the elderly. I don't think half of our mates would have got a GCSE in Maths without him. He was my friend. I wanted to be just like him. He was Batman and I was Robin.

Ben exits the bathroom. Runs into the bedroom, phone in his pocket. He smells his arm pits realises they smell and grabs a roll-on deodorant and puts it on under his t-shirt.

Ben: (*in deepest superhero mock voice*) Come Robin, the night awaits us.

Jack stands up and strikes a pose like a superhero.

Jack: (*superhero voice back*) Yes Batman, (*picking up bag*) let's party.

Ben: (*with a smile*) But first follow me.

Jack: (*to audience, normal voice*) Ben was well known for his mischief too. The plan for tonight had begun earlier in the day at school.

End Scene. Fade to black.

Scene 3: Plotting

School bell rings. Desks for each of the students Mia, Jordon, Taylor, Charlie, Ali, Ben and Jack share a desk. The teacher has their back to the class and is writing on the board, wittering about Shakespeare's Macbeth and the role of fate in the play.

Jordon's phone noisily vibrates and s/he takes it out of their pocket. Jordon seems to scan through the phone. Jordon's face lights up and then s/he writes a message on a piece of paper, which is passed around the class. Each student is excited when the note is read. The note is finally passed to Ben and Jack's table.

The teacher turns to see what the commotion is.

Teacher: Will you please continue with your work, quietly?

Class: Yes Miss/Mr Anderson.

Jack: What's the note say? It's not another one of Jordon's drawings of miss/sir naked again is it?

Ben unfolds the paper.

Ben: Secret party tonight. Location to be confirmed. You up for it?

They both turn around to look at the rest of class. The other students put their thumbs up and wink. Teacher turns around.

Teacher: Will you lot concentrate?

The bell rings.

Teacher: (*under their breath*) Thank God it's Friday. (*to the class*) Class dismissed.

The teacher leaves quickly, as the students in the class crowd round Jack and Ben.

Taylor: Soo you up for tonight?

Charlie: Sounds like it could be fun.

Ali: You two losers coming?

Jack: Where exactly is it?

Jordon: It's a secret, durggh. We get told later where it is and we just turn up.

Ben: Sounds like a rave?

Jordon: Nahh it says it's a party.

Mia: I'm game if you two are?

Jack and Ben look at each other.

Jack: I've got nothing planned tonight.

Ben: I'm meant to be helping out at the care home tomorrow. I probably shouldn't.

Ali: (*mocking*) 'I'm working at the care home'. Live a little, you're sixteen not sixty. You're not dead yet!

Taylor: Come on guys, we can get some booze, get our dancing shoes on.

Ben: Sounds great!

Jordon: Everyone meet at nine at the station. Bring your money and I'll get the gear.

The group say bye to each other leaving Mia, Ben and Jack who are finishing packing up.

Mia: Are you really gonna put on your dancing shoes guys?

Jack: (*innocently*) I just thought I'd wear trainers. You think we need to wear smart shoes?

Mia: No, you dorks! Dancing shoes is another name for E!

The pair look at each other blankly.

Mia: Gear, Candy, Skittles, XTC, Vitamin E... They're talking about ecstasy.

Jack and Ben: Oh crap!

Mia: You going to do it then?

Jack: No way! I ain't messing with no drugs.

Ben: Yeah I might. You going to Mia?

Mia: Yeah I might if you do Ben.

Jack: Come on, we can't be playing with that stuff.

Ben: Like Ali said, I'm not dead yet.

End scene. Fade to black.

Scene 4: Erm, Mum

Ben has a Fruit Shoot bottle and a small water bottle with him. Jack has a bag on his back. Ben stuffs the water in his bag. The pair are in front of a cupboard that has a bottle of alcohol spirits in it.

Ben: Drink this up will you?

Ben passes the bottle of Fruit Shoot and Jack begins to down it. Ben then goes into the cupboard, pulls out a bottle of spirit and takes the lid off the bottle. Ben takes a quick swig.

Jack: What's that for?

Ben: Take the lid off that will you?

19

Jack unscrews the lid of Fruit Shoot and Ben pours in the spirit.

Mum: (*calls from offstage*) Ben, Jack have you left yet?

Ben: Bugger! Put it away!

Jack: Bloody hell!

The pair quickly put everything away as Mum walks into the room.

Mum: What are you two up to?

Jack and Ben: Nothing.

Mum: Uh huh?

Ben: Jack just wanted a Fruit Shoot before we go out.

Jack: Yeah, super thirsty.

Mum: Oh really?

Ben: Yup.

Mum: So where are you two off to tonight?

Ben: (*looks at Jack*) We're going out...

Jack: We're going for a sleepover at Andy's.

Mum: A sleepover, I see.

Ben: A sleepover at Andy's (*glaring at Jack*), just a few friends having fun together.

Mum: Well I hope you two have fun.

Jack and Ben begin to leave.

Jack: Have a good night Jane.

Mum: You keep each other safe. (*calls back for Ben.*) Ben?

Ben: I'll be out in a minute.

Jack walks to go off stage, but waits in the corner watching as they say goodbye.

Ben: What Mum?

Mum: I just wanted to tell you I love you, and not to forget to brush your teeth before bed.

Ben: Yes Mum, I love you too.

(Mum and Ben hug and freeze.)

Jack: (*to the audience*) If only she knew. Would she have held on longer? Would he have said something different? That, we will never know.

Mum and Ben unfreeze.

Jack: (*reluctantly*) Come on Ben.

Ben: See you later, Mum.

The pair walk off. Mum waves.

Mum: Hope you remembered some fresh boxers, Benjamin!

Ben: (*from offstage*) You're so embarrassing!

End scene. Fade to black.

Scene 5: The Walk

Ben and Jack are walking and discussing the night's plans. Sounds of light traffic are heard as they walk.

Ben: So, I messaged my brother and he thinks it sounds like a rave.

Jack: Aren't those things illegal?

Ben: (*nervous*) Nah! I'm sure it'll be great fun. Music, dancing...

Jack: (*being sarcastic*) Sounds great fun, crappy music, in a muddy field, with you lot off your faces.

Ben: Why so serious? Come on, we're sixteen! The world is at our feet.

Ben stops and looks at Jack.

Ben: Let's live whilst we're young.

Jack: Did you just quote One Direction?

Ben: Shut up!

Ben begins walking again and Jack joins him

Jack: (*taking the mickey*) Oh Harry! I'm your biggest fan. Sign my butt!

Daniel's phone receives a message.

Ben: Ah crap! Mia ain't coming tonight.

Jack: What? Call her!

Mia appears at a corner of the stage. Ben calls Mia

Mia: Hello?

Ben: What's going on?

Mia: Sorry Ben. I couldn't find the keys to my house. I just got in. I won't get to you in time.

Ben: That's rubbish!

Mia: You go have fun though. You can tell me all about it.

Ben: Alright then!

Mia: I'm at the end of the phone if you need me.

Ben: Catch you later.

Mia: Bye.

Ben ends the call, puts phone in his pocket. Mumbles under his breath.

Ben: (*Mocking*) 'I'm at the end of the phone if you need me.' (*Looking back to Jack*) Well, it looks like it's just you and me then. Batman and Robin in The Night to Remember.

Jack: You won't remember anything if you do what they're planning.

Ben: No one's making me do anything I don't want to. Come on, let's meet up with them and see what the night has in store.

Jack; (*to audience*) I wish there really was just a sleepover at Andy's. That we could just go there, play Xbox and live whilst we're young.

Ben: (*Frustrated*) Hurry up.

End scene. Fade to black.

Scene 6: Crossing the Tracks

The group of Jordon, Taylor, Charlie and Ali are waiting at the train station. As Ben and Jack arrive the group cheer and say hello to each other. Train station noises are heard overhead.

Taylor: Good evening gentlemen. Ready to party?

Ali: You got the cash?

Ben: Yeah I got some.

Ali: What about you Jack?

Jack: Not for me thanks.

Charlie: Wimp.

Jack: Whatever.

Jordon: Alright! Aliright! Chill. Jack can be our lookout. Always good to have someone sober.

Ali: So, how much you want? 1gram, half an ounce, 8 ball, pack, bundle, quarter of an ounce?

Charlie: Get him a brick?

All laugh, except Ben and Jack who are confused by the comments.

Ben: What you guys having?

Taylor: Not sure. Will see what the best deal is. Give Ali the cash and we'll be right back.

Ben hands over the cash

Ali: Love it. Be right back.

Ali and Taylor walk off.

Charlie and Jordon go into one of their bags and open a can of beer and start swigging.

Jack walks to the end of the stage and beckons Ben over.

Jack: Are you really sure you want to do this?

Ben: I've bought it now.

Jack: But it's drugs Ben. You don't know where those two are getting it from.

Ben: I'm sure they know where they are getting it from.

Jack: Ali can't even count to twenty without taking off his/her shoes. I have a horrible feeling about this. Let's cut the cash and go home.

Ben: But they're all doing it.

Jack: So let them do what they wanna do. Ben come on.

Ali and Taylor walk back on stage.

Taylor: We got the stuff.

Ali: Let's get this party started!

Charlie: Let's see it! Let's see it!

Jordon: Which one's mine? It all looks the same.

Ali: Erm, I don't know. I just gave them the money and they gave me these.

Ali shows five packets with white powder. Similar amounts seem to be in them all.

Taylor: I said you should have gone Jordon.

Charlie: Whatever, everyone just take a bag.

They each take a pack and line up along the stage. They each hold up and inspect their packet.

Jordon: Ladies and gentlemen, get your water.

The four except Ben pull out from their bags a 1.5 litre bottle, and Ben gets a 500ml bottle from Jack's bag.

Ben and Jack look at everyone's bottle size.

Charlie: Pour.

They put the white powder into their bottles and shake them.

They each look at their bottles. A train sound approaches, the same sound effect is used as at the beginning of the play.

Jordon: Guys we're really doing this?

Ben: I'm not sure...I...

Taylor: Stop being such a baby!

Charlie: Its good stuff, I promise.

Everyone unscrews the lids of their bottles. Ben more reluctantly.

Ali: We're all going to do it. Come on!

Ben: Okay! Okay!

The group cheers.

Jack: Are you sure you want to do this?

Ben: Come on Jack, what's the worst that could happen?

Ali, Charlie, Taylor, Jordon: Three, two, one... Go!

The four take a small swig whilst Ben takes a large mouthful. The cast freeze mid swig.

Jack: *(to audience)* From that moment the timer began.

A clock/timer begins a countdown of three days-seventy two hours, either a physical clock or a visual in the theatre. The cast unfreeze.

Taylor: Well look at Mr Hardcore, taking a big swig!

Charlie: It'll start working soon, don't you worry.

Jordon's phone beeps.

Jordon: Yes mate! The location's just been released for the rave!

Jack: I thought you said it was a party?

Charlie: The party of your life, mate!

Ali: Party? Rave? Who cares?

Ben: It's not too far away is it? I don't want to be too late.

Charlie: (*mocking*) 'I don't want to be too late!' Alright Cinderella!

Jack: (*pulling Ben aside*) We don't have to go Ben, we can go home.

Ben: It's a bit late now.

Taylor: (*interrupting*) That train is just about to leave.

Jordon: Are you going to drink any more of that?

Group, all except Jack, start cheering Ben's name. A couple of them aren't sure.

Jack: Don't do it Ben.

Ben looks at the group and then finishes the bottle. The group cheers.

Jordon: Woah I didn't mean all of it!

Jordon pats Ben on the back and heads to the train. Ben is a bit dazed by what he has just done.

Overhead a whistle blows.

Jack: (*to audience*) He really shouldn't have done that.

Ben: Jack, will you keep an eye on me?

Jack: Of course, Batman. You sure you wanna go?

Ben: (*pause*) Yeah. Come on Robin.

Voiceover 'Please stand clear of the closing doors' and beep. The sound of the train leaving is heard and fades out.

End scene. Fade to black.

Scene 7: Last Dance

A deep rave bass ignites the stage. Flashing lights and images. There are a couple of people propped up on stage and a pulsating group dance in the middle.

The group of Ben, Jack, Ali, Charlie, Jordon and Taylor are in a queue. Jack has his bag on his back. Ben looks a bit sweaty already. A bouncer is letting the guys in one by one.

Jack: (*shouting to the audience across the noise*) As soon as we got off the train I could hear the bass. I already had a feeling in the pit of my stomach that something was not quite right.

Jack speaks to Ben.

Jack: You alright mate?

Ben: Yes mate, I'm good. Just a bit hot.

The line has moved forward so that Jack is now in the front of the queue.

Bouncer: Open your bag please.

Jack: What?!

Bouncer: Open the bag.

Jack opens his bag and the bouncer goes through it. The only thing he pulls out is a roll on Lynx Africa.

Bouncer: Sorry, not taking this in. Pay up.

Jack disgruntledly pays up. Ben gets patted down, and waves to the bouncer as they leave.

Jack: He took my bloody Lynx Africa. I only got it yesterday.

Ben: Shut up and let's dance.

For thirty seconds they dance but you can see Jack's heart is not in it.

Jack then stops and comes to stage left. Ben follows.

Ben: What's up mate?

Jack: I'm just not feeling it.

Ben: Come on!!

Jack: I'll stay here and be home base. You have fun.

Ben drapes himself over Jack. The drugs have now kicked in.

Ben: (*slurring slightly but doing his superhero voice*) You stay here and look after the bat cave Robin!

Jack: Yes Batman...Get off, you sweaty mess.

Ben hugs Jack round the neck and places a big kiss on Jack's cheek.

Ben: You know I love you man!

Jack: How much did you take? Go dance.

Ben runs off into the mass of people. Jack awkwardly checks his phone. And taps along with his foot.

Jack: (*to audience*) The night was rubbish. The place was hot, it stunk. Something just felt wrong about the whole thing. It went past 3am and I hadn't seen Ben for a while.

Ali and Taylor come over.

Ali: Have you seen Ben? I've not seen him for ages.

Jack: No I've not seen him. I'll go look for him.

The crowd pulsates and moves as Jack and Ben miss each other. Each time Ben appears he seems more disorientated, sweaty and beginning to look lost. The music pulsates louder to its climax. As the music climaxes, Ben calls out for Jack. Ben collapses at the front of the stage. The countdown is still running.

A member of the dance group notices Ben and runs to the Bouncer, who carries Ben to the stage right. A First Aider comes over and begins checking Ben's vitals.

First Aider: Mate, can you hear me? What's your name?

Ben: (*slipping in and out of consciousness*) Jack... Jack.

First Aider: Jack! Jack? Can you hear me? Jack? Jack can you speak to me? JACK!

Jack from across the stage is calling for Ben and hears his name in reply. Jack runs to Ben's side.

Jack: (*to the audience over the music*) At 4am I finally found Ben. (*back into the story*) Oh my God. Ben! Ben, you all right mate?

First Aider: Do you know this kid?

Jack: Yeah, he's my mate.

First Aider: You know what he's taken? How much?

Jack: I think he took some ecstasy. I don't know how much.

First Aider: Look, I need you to try to get in contact with his parents. He's going to need to go to hospital.

Music begins to warp with the sound of a siren.

Jack: (*to audience*) I phoned everyone I knew. I didn't have his Mum's number or house number. I managed to get hold of his girlfriend and Mia who tried to phone his Mum.

First Aider and Bouncer lift Ben up towards side where flashing blue light is.

First Aider: Do you want to come with him in the ambulance to hospital?

All music and noise stops. Countdown still goes.

Jack: No! He'll be alright.

End scene. Fade to black.

Scene 8: Waiting

Jack is on his own crouched in a corner. In the middle of the stage is Ben. He is in a hospital bed wired up and with a breathing mask on. Alone. The clock is still counting down. We hear the beep of the machines.

Jack: I went home. I woke up the next morning expecting a selfie from Ben with some hot nurse, but nothing came. Ben's parents were woken up at five in the morning by the police.

Mum and Dad enter. Mum collapses by Ben's side in the hospital. Dad brushes his hand through Ben's hair and crouches down by Mum sobbing.

His parents were taken to the hospital to be with Ben. I stayed at home. I didn't want to get into trouble. It was just meant to be another night out.

A doctor walks in. Ben's parents stand up. When they hear about his organ failure, Mum gasps.

The amount of drugs Ben had taken was too strong for his body. He had taken a dose that was deadly enough to kill him twelve times over. The strength of the drugs meant that his body temperature had risen to forty-two degrees. At that temperature, your organs start failing.

Ben's brother enters. His Mum and Dad hug him and take him to his brother's bedside.

Ben's brother was called home from university to be with him. Ben was meant to be going to stay with him the next weekend.

A doctor comes in and shakes his head. Ben's parents cry, his brother just stares at Ben, holding his hand.

I didn't want to get in trouble. Even when I heard that the family had been told that it was a

96 percent chance he wasn't going to make it, I still hung on to that 4 percent.

I'd always thought that when someone went into hospital they came out. It didn't seem a possibility that...it could happen.

My body felt like it was preparing for Ben to go but my head wouldn't process it...It couldn't happen...my best friend couldn't...no... *(Jack can't finish the sentence).*

Everything goes very quiet as the machine slowly stops and flat lines. The timer stops. Jack cries into his arms. All that is heard is Jack's sobs.

End scene. Fade to black.

Scene 9: Message from the Family

Read by Mother – either to audience or voice over

Ben died aged sixteen. He was the loveliest boy. It is impossible to sum up such an amazing and rich character in just a few words. Ben was smart, kind and cheeky. He had a strong sense of justice, was passionate about issues of right and wrong, and he had ambitions to join the army and then to be an English teacher. He loved drama, playing the guitar, playing golf, playing Xbox and being with his friends. Thinking about the adult he would become, it was very exciting to see the potential he was displaying for the person we knew he could have been. He engaged everyone he met, and those of us who lived with him have had our lives enriched by his presence.

Whilst deeply regretting the years that no longer lie ahead, we can all take comfort from the sixteen years in which he grasped every opportunity to experience as much of life as he could. Sleep well my precious Ben.

End Scene. Fade to black.

Scene 10: Final message

Jack is now on stage on his own in the middle of the spotlight.

Jack: My best friend died when we were just sixteen. Ben died of an overdose from drugs that he did not understand and felt pressured to take. Ben wasn't some drug addict - he was just a kid with his whole future ahead of him. The first time you take drugs can be your last.

I told Ben's Mum and Dad everything. They instantly forgave me. The hardest part was telling my parents that I had been at the rave with Ben after saying I wasn't. I should have told them the truth sooner. Sorry Mum and Dad. I was just a scared kid. I didn't know what would happen to Ben.

If I had the chance to go back to that night, I would have tried my best to change Ben's mind and stop him. If only he had not taken the drugs …I should have tried harder.

I have so many regrets from that night. My biggest is that I didn't go in the ambulance with you Ben. Just to be with you for those last few hours so you weren't alone. I should have never let you go alone. I should have been there. I let you down. My job was to look after you and I didn't. I failed you.

Ben steps into the spotlight behind Jack and places a hand on his shoulder. Shakes his head showing he disagrees.

I will live my life Ben, in the hope that one day we can be reunited. Be Batman and Robin again. Ben, know that you are remembered, and I will always remember you. One last thing Ben. I love you too man. You are and always will be…my best friend.

End scene. Fade to black.

Every time a book is sold, royalties are paid to the Foundation to reinvest back into its work to inform and educate young people to enable them to make safer, informed choices

If you would like to donate or find out more about the Daniel Spargo-Mabbs Foundation, please scan the QR code below.

Supporting Resources

'I wish I'd known – Young People, Drugs and Decisions' (Sheldon Press, 2021)

by Fiona Spargo-Mabbs

This award-winning title combines Dan's story with accessible, practical information and advice targeted at parents and carers. For example, it provides 'talking points' to open conversations at home around drugs and alcohol. The book encapsulates everything Fiona wishes she had known before her son died (hence the title) with the hope others may avoid similar situations by being better informed. It won the Gold Medal for Parents and Families in the 2022 Nautilus Book Awards.

Three sets of supplementary materials have been published to accompany 'I Wish I'd Known.', available online from, Amazon, the John Murray Learning Library and via the DSM Foundation website:

Drugs Decisions and Difference is for parents of neurodiverse young people and professionals working with them;

Schools, Colleges, Drugs and Decisions is for teachers and education professionals;

Faith, Drugs and Decisions is written for Christian parents and church leaders.

Talking the Tough Stuff with Teens: Making Conversations. (Sheldon Press 2022).

by Fiona Spargo-Mabbs

Fiona's second book for parents is a practical handbook to enable parents and carers to make sense of why conversations can go awry, how to prevent that from happening and what to do if it does. The book covers everything from curfews to screen time to sex, self-harm, and suicide. It is a warm, compassionate, insightful book which every parent and carer should read. It draws on lived experience through the lens of young people and how they are rather than what others perceive them to be.

'I Love You, Mum – I Promise I Won't Die.'
(Bloomsbury 2017).

by Mark Wheeller

In May 2014, just months after Dan died, the
DSM Foundation commissioned award-winning
playwright Mark Wheeller to write a verbatim
play about what happened to him. The title uses
Dan's last words to his mother Fiona, before he
left home for what turned out to be the last time:
'I Love You, Mum – I Promise I Won't Die'.

In March 2016 the play had its first public
performances, in Southampton and London,
with its premiere at the BRIT school, just a mile
from Dan's home in Croydon. From September
2022 it has been a GCSE Drama set text
(Eduqas).

What Could Go Wrong? (Amazon 2023)

by Mark Harrington

Daniel is a happy seventeen-year old-boy, intelligent, popular, and with a loving family and friends. What could go wrong? See how one choice can change the life of Daniel and his friends and family forever.

Designed for SEND students with the cognitive age of 8+, 'What could go wrong?' is designed to teach the most vulnerable in society the dangers of drugs and alcohol use. A scheme of work and worksheets are available via the DSM Foundation website to accompany the play.

About the Author

Mark Harrington is a special needs teacher, husband, dad and dreamer. He is based in West Sussex and this is part of a new series of books and resources he is developing for SEND students. For further projects that Mark is working on please look on social media @harrington_projects or www.harringtonprojects.co.uk

harrington_projects

Notes

Printed in Great Britain
by Amazon